Beginner's Guide to

Google Drive

by

Barrie "Baz" Roberts

Learn

Google Workspace

& Apps Script

Table of Contents

1: Google Apps - What are they?

Before we dive into Google Drive, let's take a quick look at all the main Google Apps, which form part of Google Workspace.

What are they?

Basically, they are a collection of programs which do specific jobs. The first three resemble the three most widely-used programs of the Microsoft suite, i.e. Word, Excel and PowerPoint.

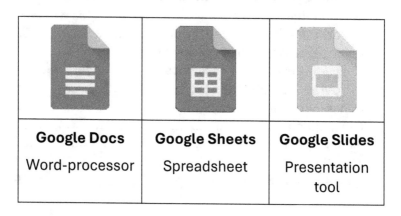

Google Docs	Google Sheets	Google Slides
Word-processor	Spreadsheet	Presentation tool

Google Drive	**Google Forms**	**Google Sites**
The space in the 'cloud' where the documents live.	Easy-to-make forms, questionnaires, and quizzes.	Create your own websites.
Google Calendar	**Gmail**	**Google Tasks**
Shareable calendar	The famous email	Organise your life with tasks.

So, what are the advantages of using these?

Collaboration: You can work on the same document at the same time as your colleagues. So, no having to email documents around.

Always at the latest revision: All the document changes are live and can be seen by all those with access to the file. So, everyone sees the latest version of the document.

Access to every change: The document continually saves and stores every revision in the cloud. This means you can go back to any revision, right back to when the file was first made.

Files and folders shared with ease: Files and folders can be private, shared with specific people, or shared with anyone with a link.

Latest software version: The software is continually updated and you always use the latest version.

It's free!: You get all the apps for free and 15Gb of Drive space in the cloud, which can be expanded.

Your beloved Microsoft Office documents can be viewed and edited within Drive or if you want you can convert them to Google Apps.

How do I get these?

You'll need to set up an account with Google (free) and you will receive full use of all the Apps mentioned above automatically. See chapter 3 for details of how to set up an account.

2: Google Drive - How does it work?

Now let's turn our attention to Google Drive which is central to most of these apps. Here's a brief explanation of what Google Drive is and how it works. It's important to have an overall understanding of how it works before diving into the details.

When you log into Google Drive, your computer connects to the place where your files are stored. This is 'in the cloud', which is actually a physical storage place somewhere in the world, in this case run by Google. Your files are basically sitting on a computer somewhere else and not physically on your computer taking up space, but you can open and edit them whenever you want.

My Google Drive
in the 'cloud'

My computer

Even though my files are on another computer, only I have access to them until I decide to share them with someone. To do that, I tell the computer who I want to share it with, in this case my friend Bob, and the computer allows access to that particular file. Bob now has access to that particular file but the file stays on my Google Drive and uses up my storage space, not his.

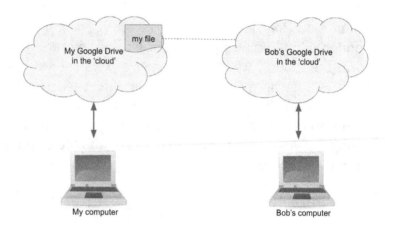

This is great but what happens if you want to share lots of files? It would be just a tad tedious sharing lots of individual files, wouldn't it? Well, there's a better way.

You can also share a folder, which contains lots of files. It has the added advantage that if you add another file in the shared folder, it automatically gets shared with the people you shared it with.

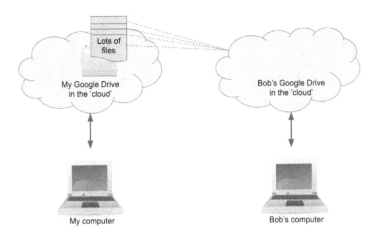

The beauty of having a drive in the cloud is that you can access your files, not only from your computer, but from any device that allows you access to Google Drive. For example, from your mobile, tablet, or work computer.

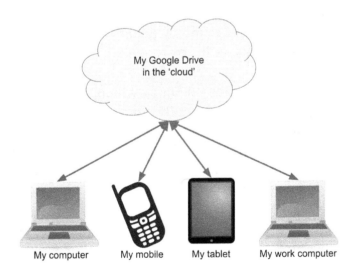

If Bob has shared some files with me, I can also access them from whatever device I have.

Google Apps like Google Docs, Google Sheets and Google Slides have some extra benefits which apart from the sharing in the cloud, make these fantastic tools to use.

Editing a file at the same time
You can open a file and edit it at the same time as other people, possibly others in a team you work with. Google automatically saves all the changes made by all the people, so the document is always up-to-date with the latest changes and you don't have to wait for one person to make a change, then another to do theirs.

An example of this is at our academy where the teachers used to have to email the students' exam results, then the coordinator would have to enter all of them into Excel. That spreadsheet would then be emailed back out to the teachers and admin. Any further changes meant the whole process had to be repeated.

Now, there is one Google Sheet, which all the teachers and admin have access to. The teachers enter the exam results on the same sheet and can do it at the same time. Meanwhile, admin have access to the sheet, meaning they have access to that information, as soon as the teachers enter it. So, no duplication of work, and no out-of-date sheets!

3: How to set up a Google account

You'll need a Google account to access your Google Drive, etc. Below are step-by-step instructions on how to set one up.

Go to **google.com** and search for "create Google account".

Google

Create a Google Account

Enter your name

First name

Last name (optional)

Next

Google

Basic information

Enter your birthday and gender

Month   Day   Year

Gender

Why we ask for birthday and gender

Next

Enter your name and surname, then click "Next". Enter your birthday and gender. Then click "Next".

Google

Choose your Gmail address

Pick a Gmail address or create your own

○ bazroberts15@gmail.com

○ robertsbaz254@gmail.com

○ Create your own Gmail address

Use your existing email   Next

It suggests a couple of email addresses you could use or you can create your own one, which you're most likely going to do.

Here, you could also use an existing email which doesn't have to be a Gmail one. As creating a Google account doesn't mean you have to use Gmail.

I'm going to create a new Gmail address. Click "Next".

Create a Gmail address
bazroberts24   @gmail.com

You can use letters, numbers & periods

Use your existing email   Next

Enter a password and enter an alternative email you can use in case you get locked out (optional).

Google

Create a strong password

Create a strong password with a mix of letters,
numbers and symbols

Password

Confirm

☐ Show password

Next

Google

Add recovery email

The address where Google can contact you if
there's unusual activity in your account or if you get
locked out.

Recovery email address

Next   Skip

You can. Add a phone number, which is useful for account security, where it can send you a code when trying to log into your account (optional).

13

Google

Add phone number

[flag ▼] | Phone number

Google will use this number only for account security. Your number won't be visible to others. You can choose later whether to use it for other purposes.

| Next | Skip |

Now, you need to set up the account. You can just choose the default settings (Express), which you can change later on or set the ones you want (Manual).

Google

Review your account info

You can use this email address to sign in later

B Baz Roberts
bazroberts24@gmail.com

Next

Google

Choose your settings

○ **Express (1 step)**
Choose your settings in one step. Your choices to turn settings on or off help tailor the content and ad experiences you see.

○ **Manual (4 steps)**
Choose your settings step by step. Your choices to turn settings on or off help tailor the content and ad experiences you see.

You can change your settings anytime at account.google.com

Next

Accept your settings by clicking "Accept All". Then confirm them by clicking "Confirm".

Google

Choose your settings

Depending on your choice, your data will be used to give you more personalized experiences and more control over the personalized ads you see

Web & App Activity
Provides things like faster searching, more relevant results, and more helpful app and content recommendations.
Learn more about Web & App Activity

15

Confirm your settings

You can change your settings anytime in your
Google Account

 Web & App Activity
This setting will be on

Finally, agree to the terms and conditions by clicking "I agree". This will open your account and your account is now set up!

You can sign out by clicking on the circle icon in the top right-hand corner and clicking "Sign out".

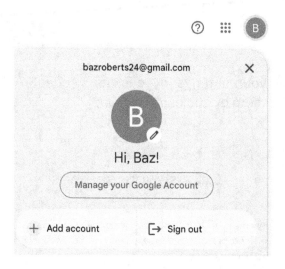

Note, Google sometimes changes what it asks for during this sign-up process, so you may see different screens.

4: How to access Google Drive

So, you've now got a Google account, how do you access your Google Drive and its contents?

Go to www.google.com. In the top right-hand corner, you'll see a blue "Sign In" button.

Click it and this will take you to the Google sign in page.

Google

Sign in

Use your Google Account

Email or phone

Forgot email?

Not your computer? Use Guest mode to sign in privately.
Learn more

Create account   Next

Type in your username. Then click "Next".

Email or phone

bazroberts24

Tip: The part before "@gmail.com" in your Gmail address is your username. You don't need to write *@gmail.com*. For example, if your email address was *bazroberts24@gmail.com* > just type in: *bazroberts24*.

Then, type in your password and click "Next".

Hi Baz

B bazroberts24@gmail.com ⌄

Enter your password

You're now logged in to your account! :) Now, where's that Drive?

Gmail   Images   ⦂⦂⦂   B

In the top right-hand corner, next to "Images", you'll see nine little dots. Click on it and a menu will open. Then, click on the Drive icon.

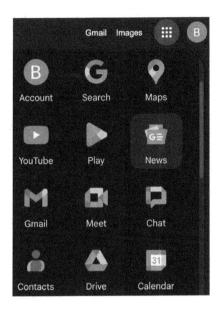

This will open your Google Drive.

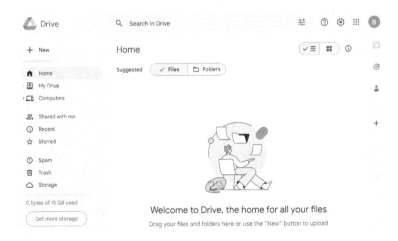

You can also access Drive by going to **drive.google.com**.

If you're not logged in, this will take you to the log in screen and then once logged in will take you directly to the Drive screen, so you won't have to select it from the menu.

Tip: I bookmark the drive.google.com page in the bookmarks menu, so I can just click on it and it takes me straight to the log in page.

If you've accessed your account on this computer before, you should see your account as one of the options. Click on it and you'll just need to enter your password and click "Next" to enter your Drive.

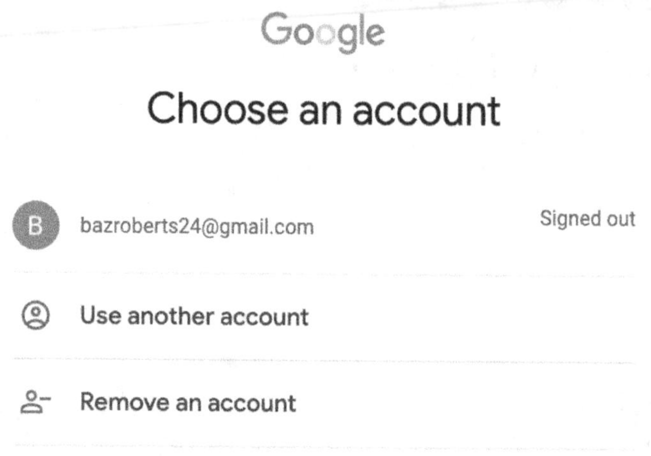

Google

Choose an account

B   bazroberts24@gmail.com   Signed out

Ⓥ   Use another account

👤–   Remove an account

If it's not there, click on "Use another account". Then, on the next screen, type in your email address, then click "Next". This takes you to the password screen. Type in your password and click "Next". You'll be taken to your Drive as before.

5: Tour of Drive

Once you've logged in to your account and clicked on Drive, you'll be presented with the main Drive page. Let's take a look around and get a feel for the layout. There are 4 main areas:

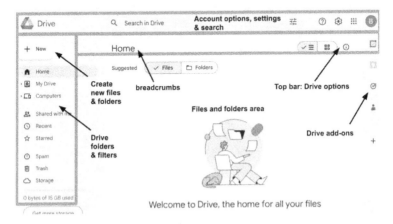

Welcome to Drive, the home for all your files

1) On the left, you have Drive folders and filters.

2) In the middle is where you will see your files and folders.

3) Above that there are Drive options and this is where you'll be able to see where your file lives in Google Drive, via a 'breadcrumbs' route, i.e. a list of the folders and sub-folders, showing where the file is.

4) At the top, there is a search box and where the account options, settings, and help are.

1) Main menu

New: Clicking on the 'New' button, will open a menu with the following options:

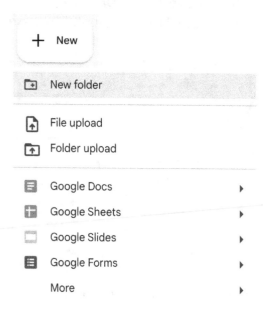

It gives you the option of:

New folder: Creates a new folder

File upload: Uploads a file from your computer

Folder upload: Uploads a complete folder from your computer, this can save you a lot of time when uploading your files to Drive.

Google Docs/Sheets/Slides/Forms: Creates a new Google Doc, Google Sheet, Google Slide, or Google Form. Workspace accounts will also see "Google Vids".

More: Opens another menu, where you can create a new Drawing, Site, My Maps, or Google Apps Script program and where you can add further Apps to Drive.

Below the New button you have the main menu:

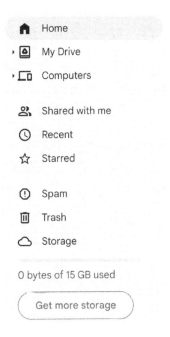

Home: Drive will suggest files and folders that it thinks you will want to use based on your history of using them.

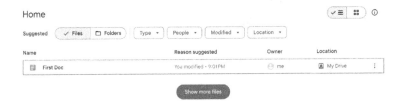

23

My Drive: This is the top-level folder in your drive, all files and folders are connected to this.

Computers: You can connect a computer to your Drive, so that the files on the computer are automatically synced to your Drive. Those files and folders are shown here.

Shared with me: One of the beauties of Google Drive is the ability to share files and folders very easily and those you share them with, will have access to the same versions as you have.

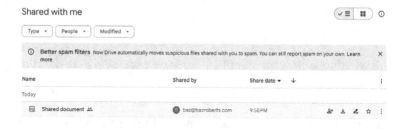

Recent: This sorts your files and folders into date order, with the most recently accessed at the top, which can be a great way to quickly access files you've recently been working on.

Recent

Type ▾	People ▾	Modified ▾

Name

Today

📄 First Doc   9:01PM   ⋮

Starred: You have the option of 'starring' your most used or most important files and folders and this filter shows all the starred ones in one place.

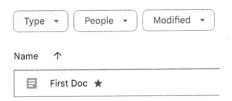

Starred

Type ▾	People ▾	Modified ▾

Name ↑

📄 First Doc ★

Spam: If Drive detects someone has shared a file with you and thinks it's spam, it will appear here.

Trash: If you delete something, it goes in here. It stays here for 30 days and then will be deleted or it will be permanently deleted if you manually empty the trash.

Trash for My Drive

Type ▾	Modified ▾

Items in trash will be deleted forever after 30 days   Empty trash

Name	Owner

Today

📄 First Doc   🔵 me   ⋮

Storage: This will show you how much storage you're using and how much is used by Drive, Photos, and Gmail. Plus, it will show you the files using the most storage.

A free account will give you 15Gb, which is plenty for the average user, but there are options to increase this. If you need more, click on 'Get more storage'.

Get Drive for desktop: Finally, on the bottom-left, you have the option to install Google Drive onto your PC or Mac. This copies all your files locally onto your computer. This is a good option for backing up files and for editing non-Google files.

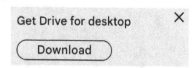

Shared Drives: You might see an extra menu under "My Drive" if either you have a Workspace account, or if someone has shared a Shared Drive with you. These are drives where the files and folders are not owned by specific people but are shared between a group of users, for example, a department at work.

2) Files and folders area

With a new account, your file and folders area will be empty. Below, I've created a new Google Doc and as you can see it shows me the file and some basic details about it.

Name ↑	Owner	Last mo... ▾	File size
🗐 First Doc	🟢 me	9:01 PM	1 KB

3) Folder breadcrumbs, views, and options

Breadcrumbs

Above the files and folder area is an area where you can navigate through the folders on your Drive, and you will see 'breadcrumbs' showing you where you are in relation to the main folder. It also allows you to open a folder further up the breadcrumbs by clicking on the folder name.

Here's an example:

My Drive > Example folder ▾

Views

There are two possible views in Drive in the files and folder area, List and Grid view.

List view

'List view' shows your files as a list, plus the owner of the file, when it was last modified and the file size.

Name ↑	Owner	Last mo... ▼	File size
First Doc	me	9:01PM	1 KB

Grid view

'Grid view' which shows your files as a grid and shows you a visual preview of the contents of the file.

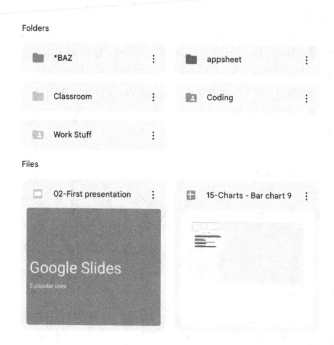

Personally, with a lot of files I find list view better, especially if you know the filename, but grid view can be useful for finding specific photos or even documents which you can't remember the exact filename for.

Sorting files and folders

Finally, you can sort the files and folders area. You can sort the files and folders by name by clicking on the arrow next to "Name" at the top of the list.

You can also sort them by the date the files were last modified, by the last time you modified them, or by the last time you opened the files. Just click on "Last modified".

Details and Activity

View details: Clicking on the (i) symbol brings up a menu with two options: Details or Activity.

View details

Clicking on a file and clicking "Details" brings up the details. It shows a preview of the contents, tells you whether it's shared with other people, the file type, file size, Drive storage used, Location: where it is on Drive, Owner: who is the owner of the file (usually the creator).

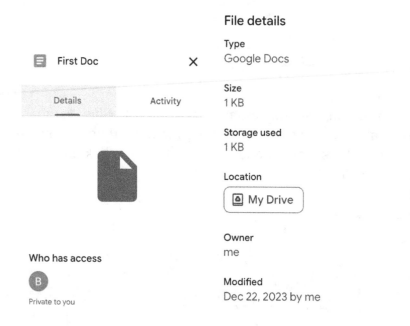

You'll also find info on when it was last modified, last opened and when it was created. It tells you if others can edit or download it. You can also add a description.

Activity

This tells you all the activity that has happened with that particular file or folder. It tells you when it was created, modified, uploaded, shared, etc and also tells you who carried out the actions.

Clicking on a folder, shows you the activity of all the files in that folder.

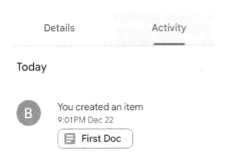

To close the Details/Activity window, click on the X at the top to the right of the file or folder name.

4) Settings, help, settings, and account options

At the top of the screen, we can find the Drive search bar, the Help menu, the Settings menu, Google Apps, and Google Account menu.

Search bar

It's no surprise that Google includes a powerful search engine so you can find your files, without having to hunt for them via the folders. Just type in the words you want and press Enter. Google will search for filenames and also, words within documents.

It also provides some filters, to enable you to find what you want more quickly and easily. Just click on the filter icon on the right-hand side of the search box.

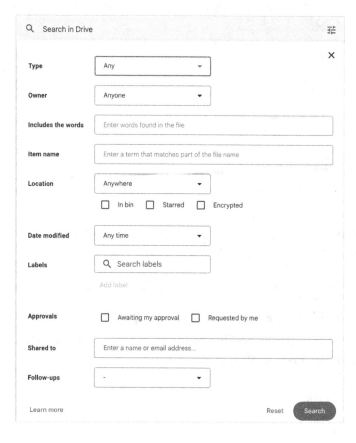

This brings up the filter menu. Select what you want to filter and click Search. More about this in Chapter 13.

Help

Clicking on the question mark opens up the help menu. You can search for help, browse help articles, and also send feedback on any problems or suggest improvements to Drive.

Settings

This gives you three options: to open the settings menu, to download "Drive for desktop" to your computer, and a list of keyboard shortcuts.

We'll look at the Settings menu in more detail in chapter 16.

5) Hidden file and folder menu

Clicking on a file or folder brings up a hidden menu just above the main file and folder area.

Share file or folder: This brings up the sharing options, to allow you to control who can access the file or folder.

Download: This downloads the file or if it's a Google file, it will download an Office-version of it.

Move: This will open the move menu, allowing you to move the file or folder.

Trash: This removes the file and puts it in the trash.

Get link: This gets the website address (URL) of the file or folder, which you can share via, for example, email. Note: To access it, the person receiving the link will need to have access rights to the file or folder. See the section on sharing files and folders.

More options: This opens more options, e.g. 'starring' the file for quick access, making a copy, etc. We'll look at this in more detail later in the book.

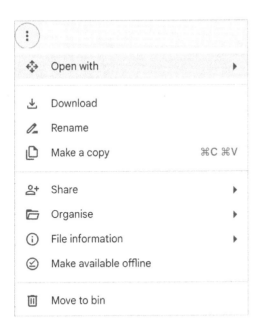

Google Apps menu

In the top-right of the screen we have a 9-dot icon, which is the Google Apps menu. Clicking on this brings up the menu to access other Google programs and options. e.g. Gmail.

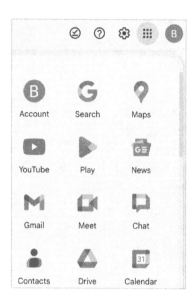

Account options

Next to the 9 dots is the account menu.

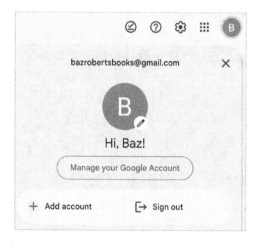

Clicking on this brings up the Google account menu. Here you can:

-change your account profile picture (click on the pencil icon in the circle)
-manage your account settings
-sign out, when you have finished using Drive. Essential if you are sharing the computer with someone else.

Clicking on "Manage your Google Account" opens your account page, where you can change things like your personal info, change your privacy settings, etc.

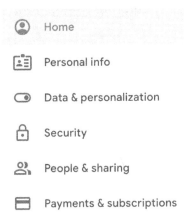

Home

Personal info

Data & personalization

Security

People & sharing

Payments & subscriptions

6: How to manage files and folders

You've got into Google Drive, now let's go through the most common actions you do with files and folders: **creating, naming, copying, and deleting**.

Creating a file

As an example, let's create a new Google Doc file.

1) Click on the "New" button on the left of the screen, which opens the menu.

2) Click the type of new document you want, in this example, click on "Google Docs".

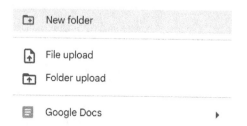

3) The new Google Doc will open in a new tab.

4) By default, the document is named "Untitled document". You can see the name in the top left-hand corner.

5) To see the file you've just created in your Google Drive. First, type something in the document. This is because Drive doesn't show your file until there is some content in there. Unlike Word, etc, there's no need to press Save, it does this automatically!

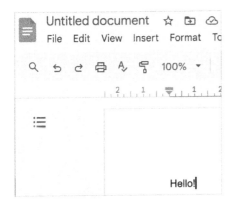

6) Then click on the Drive tab and you will see your file there, with who owns the file, the time or date it was created, and the size of the file.

Tip: There is a quick shortcut to create a Docs file if you use the Google **Chrome** browser. In the address bar, just type **doc.new** and this will open a tab like before with a new document. This file will be stored in My Drive but you can move it afterwards. Note, **docs.new** also works.

You can do the same for other Google files and apps:
sheets.new – Creates a new Google Sheets document
slides.new – Creates a new Google Slides document
forms.new – Creates a new Google form
meet.new – Opens a new Google Meet session

Creating a folder

1) Go to the same menu as above, by clicking on the New button.

2) Click on "New folder".

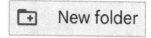

3) A box will appear asking you to name the folder. Type a name in and click the blue Create button.

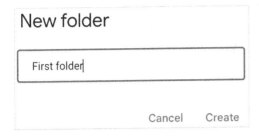

New folder

First folder|

Cancel   Create

4) In your My Drive, you'll see the newly-created folder, highlighted in blue.

First folder   me   11:58

Copying a file

1) Right click on the file you want to copy. This brings up a menu. Click on "Make a Copy".

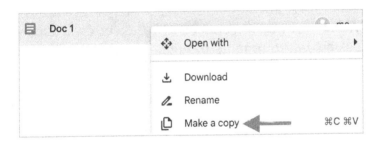

Doc 1

✥ Open with   ▶

⬇ Download

✎ Rename

🗐 Make a copy ◀━━━   ⌘C ⌘V

2) In your My Drive, you will see the new file labelled "Copy of... + the title of the original file".

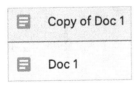

Copy of Doc 1

Doc 1

3) To rename it, right-click on it and click "Rename".

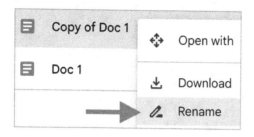

Tip: You can also rename a file by clicking on the file and pressing "N".

Alternatively, if you click on the file or folder and hover over the part to the right of the file size, a few icons will appear and you can click the rename icon.

4) Whichever way you choose to do it, a box will appear asking you to rename the file. Just type in the new name and click OK.

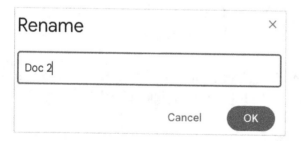

5) You'll see your renamed document highlighted in blue.

Tip: An alternative way to make a copy is to click on the file and press Ctrl + C (Cmd + C on a Mac) and Ctrl + V (Cmd + V) to copy and paste a new document. The first time you do it, you may need to give permission to allow access to your clipboard – Just click "Allow" on the pop-up message.

Deleting a file

1) Right click on the file or folder you want to delete. This will bring up a menu. Click on "Move to trash" to send it to the Trash.

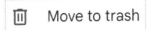

It will check if you want to do that. Just click "Move to trash" again.

This removes it from your Drive, but it is not permanently deleted. This is a useful safeguard, in case you delete it by mistake. To delete it permanently, go to the Trash.

You will see the file you just deleted, and possibly other files and folders too, as they all end up in the same trash bin. To delete all the files in the trash, click on "Empty trash".

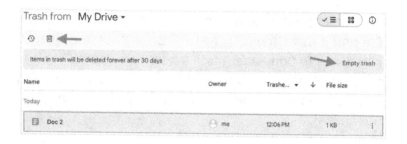

If you only want to delete a particular file, you can also right-click on it in the Trash and a menu will appear. Click "Delete forever" to do just that.

Click on "Delete forever" in the pop-up message.

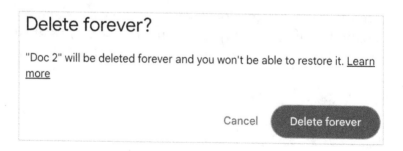

If you have removed a file by mistake, you can return files from the trash back to your My Drive, by right-clicking on the file and clicking on "Restore" from the menu.

You can also access the "Restore" and "Delete forever" options from the bar above the files and folders.

Note, the files in the trash are automatically-deleted after 30 days from being sent to the trash.

7: Moving files around

There are different ways to move files around. Below are the four main ways.

1) Drag and drop within the files and folder area

Just click on the file or folder, hold the button down and drag it to the folder you want, then let go of the mouse button.

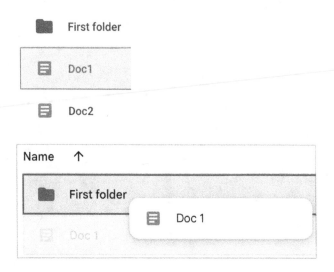

Double-clicking on the folder you just moved the file to, shows the file in its new location.

Use this technique if the folder you want to move the file to, is within the folder you're currently in.

2) Drag and drop to the left-hand side menu

In this example, I'm going to put a file that's currently in my "My Drive" and put it in a sub-folder called "First folder". Using the drag and drop technique one above won't work here as the folder is within another folder called "Book Examples", and I can't see it in the files and folder area. So, we can use the menu on the left-hand side.

On the menu on the left-hand side, you will see "My Drive". If you've already created another folder in My Drive, then you will see a little triangle to the side of My Drive.

Note: if you've just created the folder, sometimes the triangle doesn't appear straight away, if this happens, just refresh the page.

▸ 🔲 My Drive

Click on the triangle next to the My Drive icon and the next level of folders will be shown. You can do the same for other sub-folders. For example, here I have opened My Drive and the folder called "Book Examples".

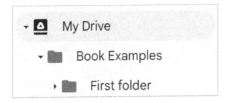

It shows me the folder in Book Examples called "First Folder" and that's the one I want, so I just click on the file or folder, hold the button down and drag it to the folder I want, then let go of the mouse button.

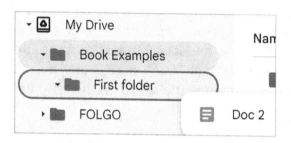

This is useful for when you want to move files and folders to other folders which are more than one level down. You can also use the left-hand menu to navigate to the folders you want.

You can also open these folders whilst dragging the file by hovering over the little triangle of each folder.

3) Drag and drop to the breadcrumbs

We can also drag and drop files and folders to a folder in the breadcrumbs.

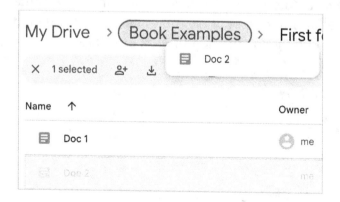

4) Hidden menu

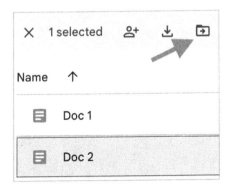

When you click on a file or folder it displays a menu at the top of the files and folder area and one of the options is to move the file or folder.

This brings up the "Move" dialogue box. It shows you the folder it's currently in and by default, brings up suggested folders it could go to.

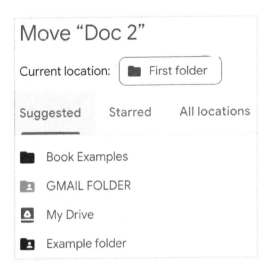

Let's put it in the "Book Examples" folder. I could just click on the Book Examples suggestion but for now ignore the suggestion and click on "All locations" as it's important to know how to find a specific folder if it's not among the suggestions, which can happen if you have lots of folders.

This always starts from My Drive. To go to the next level down of folders, click on the arrow on the right-hand side.

Now we see "Book Examples" is one of the options. To move the file here, click "Move".

If the folder you are moving it to has different access rights you will see a message asking you to confirm the move. Just click "Move" again.

You can use the above techniques for moving folders too.

If you are moving shared files or folders, be careful as this may change the access rights to them.

You can also access the Move box by right-clicking on the file or folder you want to move. This brings up a menu and then click on "Organize" > "Move".

Moving multiple files and folders

We don't need to move files or folders individually, we can move <u>multiple</u> files and folders at same time. The only difference is the way you select the files or folders you want to move.

However, this is exactly the same way you do it in Windows or MacOS, i.e. you hold Ctrl (on Windows) or Cmd (on a Mac) to select specific files, or you hold down the Shift key to select a range of files.

Click on the first file you want to move, then hold down Ctrl (or Cmd) and then click on the other files you want to move. The ones that you have chosen will be highlighted in blue.

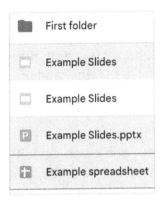

Or if the files you want are all together, click on the top one, hold down the Shift key, then click on the bottom one. All the files from the top to the bottom one will then be highlighted.

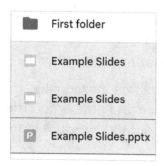

Once you have your files or folders highlighted, just drag them to the folder you want to move them to, using one of the drag and drop methods shown above.

A blue circle with the number of files you're moving will appear as you move it.

If you want to move all the files and folders within the files and folder area, just click on a file or folder and then press Ctrl and A together to select all the files and folders (Cmd + A on a Mac).

If you want to select all the files but don't want specific ones, you can select them all using Ctrl + A, let go, then holding the Ctrl key down, click on the files or folders you don't want to include. This will then deselect them.

🖼	Example Slides
🖼	Example Slides
P	Example Slides.pptx
🞢	Example spreadsheet

8: Sharing files/folders with specific people

Once you've created something often you want to share it with someone else, a team, a class or even the whole world, and Google Drive allows you to do just this.

Personally, I think this is one of the most important parts of Drive to understand well, and I know so many people that don't fully understand how sharing works on Drive, so please read this chapter and the following one carefully. Fortunately, Google has made sharing a lot simpler and clearer than it used to be.

Before looking at how it's done, let's look at the options there are.

Access options

1) Only you have access
You can keep your files & folders private on your "My Drive". By default, only you can see your file or folder.

2) Share with a specific person

Only you and Bob can see the file or folder. Bob needs to log in to his Google account to see the file or folder.

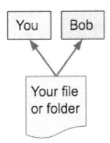

3) Share with a group of people

Only you and they can see the file or folder. They need to log in to see the file or folder. Really this is the same as the previous option, just with multiple people.

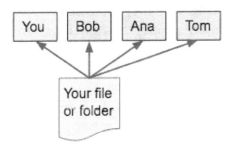

4) Give access by sharing a link

You can share your file or folder by sharing a link with them. They need this link in order to access the file or folder. It's like giving them a key to be able to open it.

Important: They don't need to log in to be able to do this. This means you don't know who has accessed your file, only that they must have done it with your link. Use with caution, as you can't control who shares that link.

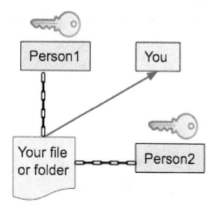

This is useful if you share the link somewhere else, e.g. a website, an email in Outlook, a blog, etc.

Permissions

Apart from giving access to your file, you also have the option of controlling what they can do within that file or folder. The three main permissions are:

Can edit - They can edit the file.

Can comment - They can't edit the file, but can leave comments in it.

Can view - They can't do either of the above, but can look at it.

Sharing a file or folder

Let's now look at how we share files and folders. We're going to share a folder as an example.

Click on the folder (or file) you want to share and you will see a menu appear on the right. Click on the "Share" icon.

You can also access the same menu by selecting your file or folder and clicking on the "Share" icon in the bar that appears above the files and folders area.

This opens the Share dialogue box. It's split into two halves:

-The top half is who you're sharing the file or folder with and what access rights they have.

-The bottom half is the type of access there is to this file or folder, e.g. is it restricted to only these particular people or anyone with the file or folder link.

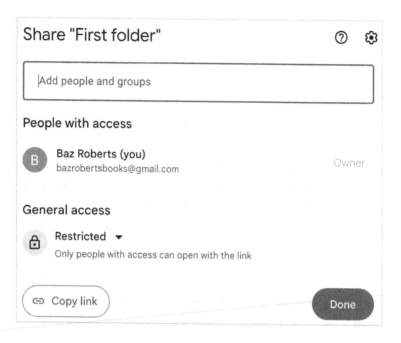

We can see that it's only restricted to me. Let's focus on the top half for now.

Let's add someone to share this folder with. Type in their email address in the box that says "Add people and groups", then press Enter.

This will change the dialogue box to a messaging box. Here, we have the option of notifying the person (or people) that we have shared the file or folder with them.

Note, you can share with multiple people, just enter an email address, press Enter, and then enter another.

If you don't want them to receive an email with this notification, untick the Notify people checkbox.

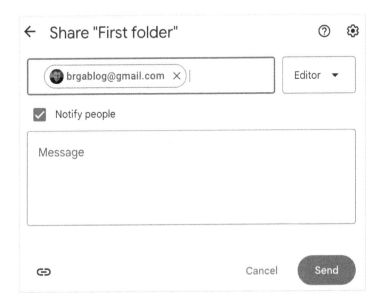

In this example, I do want to notify them, so first I want to add a little message in the Message box.

You also have the option of changing the type of permissions they have. By default, they will have Editor rights.

Click on "Editor" and you will see 3 options:

Viewer – they can only view the contents of the folder

Commenter – they can comment on documents but can't edit them. Plus, they can't share files.

Editor – They can add, remove and edit files within the folder

By default, Editor will be selected and I'll leave it like that for this example.

Then click "Send".

You will see that the folder now has a little person icon in it to show you that it's being shared.

If we select sharing again, we can see that the new person has been added and that he has Editor rights to the folder.

Making someone the new owner

Occasionally you may want to change the owner of a file or a folder. For example, if you have a new account and you want to move things to that one, or someone else now has responsibility for that document or folder.

If we click on the Editor drop-down menu we saw above, we will see that we can transfer the ownership of the file or folder. To make them the new owner, click "Transfer ownership".

A message will appear to check if you want to do it. Click "Send invitation".

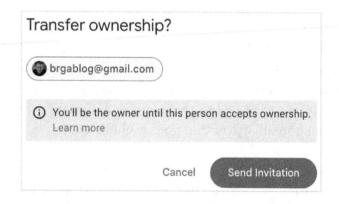

Once the person accepts, you will now see that *brgablog* is now the owner of the file and the original owner *bazrobertsbooks* is now an editor.

Back on my Drive (*bazrobertsbooks* account), I can see the folder has changed to a shortcut, as this folder isn't mine anymore and it links to *brgablog's* folder.

 First folder

You can cancel the transfer initiation from the Editor menu and click "Cancel transfer ownership".

Removing someone's access to a file or folder

To remove someone's access to a file or folder, we click on it and click the "Share" icon, as we saw above, then click on the Editor drop-down menu next to their name, and click "Remove access" and then Save.

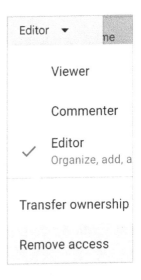

Allow/Prevent editors to change permissions & sharing

We have an extra level of control for permissions. We can allow or prevent editors from changing permissions and sharing rights.

To do so, whilst in the "Share" dialogue box, click on the cog icon in the top-right corner.

For folders, you only have one option, which by default is ticked, i.e. editors can change permissions and sharing rights.

To prevent them, untick the option, then return to the previous screen and click "Done".

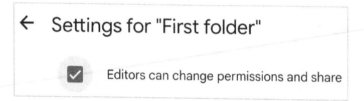

If I open the sharing box with the *brgablog* account, it will state that I'm an editor but I can't share or change the permissions without asking for permission from the folder owner.

Files have an extra setting that this last section offers an extra option, which allows us to prevent viewers and commenters from downloading, printing, or copying files.

← **Settings for "Doc 2"**

☑ Editors can change permissions and share

☑ Viewers and commenters can see the option to download, print, and copy

Share folders not files

In general, my advice is to share folders not individual files, as if you share a folder it will automatically set the same sharing permissions to all the files and folders in it, unless otherwise set individually. This makes it much easier to control and change in the future.

The great thing about sharing the files and not emailing them like in the past, is that all the users have access to the latest document and multiple users can open and **edit the file at the same time**. Google Drive saves every single change.

9: Sharing files/folders with the link

In the previous chapter, we shared our files and folders with specific people but we can also open the access to give anyone who has the link to the file or folder the ability to access it.

We might want to do that if we don't know exactly who's going to access the file or folder or maybe because it's just quicker to open the access rather than inviting everyone individually.

Changing the access to anyone with the link

Open the "Share" dialogue box as we did in the previous chapter.

You will see the dialogue box is divided into two:

- The top half is for sharing with specific people;

- The bottom half is for changing the access rights from restricted to the people above, to sharing with anyone who has the link.

We looked at the top half in the last chapter and in this chapter we're going to focus on the bottom half, titled "General Access".

There are two main things we can do here:

1) Grab a copy of the link to share it.

2) Change the general access permissions.

To get the link, click on "Copy link" and this will copy the file or folder link to the clipboard.

Note, this on its own doesn't change the permission rights. This means only the people in the sharing list above it, can open the link.

To change the access rights, click on "Restricted" and click on "Anyone with the link". This will change the access rights to anyone with the link.

By default, it will give anyone with the link <u>view</u> access only. We can see that, as it states "Anyone on the internet with this link can view". Also, on the right-hand side it states "Viewer".

We can change the access they have from View only, to comment only or editing right, by clicking on the drop-down menu and selecting one of the options.

Click "Done" to confirm your changes.

If we want to restrict it back to the specific people, click on "Anyone with the link", and then select "Restricted".

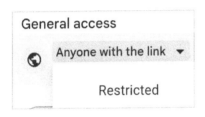

General access

🌐 Anyone with the link ▾

Restricted

How to quickly get the link to share

If you want to get the link, it's quicker to click on the file or folder and from the menu that appears above the files and folders, click on the link icon.

You will see a confirmation message and can change the access rights by clicking "Manage access", for example, to change access from "restricted" to "anyone with the link".

Link copied   Manage access   ✕

Another way if it's a Google document (Docs, Sheets, Slides, or Forms), is to open the document and copy the address from the browser address bar.

Just make sure, if you're getting the link, that the access rights are set to what you need.

Where can I find files/folders that have been shared with me?

Fortunately, Google provides us with a convenient filter that shows you all the files or folders that are shared with you.

Back on the main Drive screen, on the left-hand side, you'll see "Shared with me". Click on this to show the list of files and folders that have been shared with you.

It shows you who shared it and when. Note: by default, the filter is sorted in date order, with the most recent at the top.

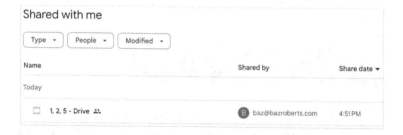

Note, as this is just a filtered list and not a folder, you can't change the order of the files or folders. You can, however, sort the list in different ways and filter it by file type, the person sharing the file, and when it was last modified.

To filter the list, click on one of the filter menus, Type, People, or Modified and enter what you want to filter it by.

70

Shared with me

To sort the list, click on the little triangle next to Share date and choose what you want to sort it by. To sort it the opposite way round, click on the arrow to the right of the menu.

Adding a sharing expiry date (Workspace only)

If you have a Workspace account, it's possible to add a sharing expiry date to the file or folder, to limit the time the user(s) have access to it. From the "Share" dialogue, click on the Editor drop-down and click "Add expiry".

This will add a default date and time to the file. To edit this, click on the pencil icon.

Then choose a date and time and click "Done".

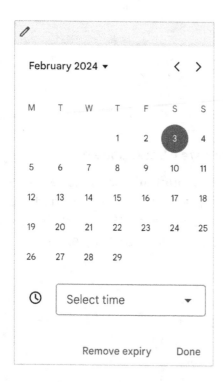

You can remove an expiry date from here by clicking "Remove expiry" and clicking "Done".

10: Quick access to your files

You may have hundreds of files on your Google Drive, but if you're like me, you end up only using certain ones all the time.

Drive has a couple of options to help you get to those files or folders quickly.

- Starring files and folders

- Home page suggestions

- Changing colours of folders

- Shortcuts

Starring files and folders

Google Drive has the option to "star" them, so that they appear in the "Starred" filter.

Click on the file or folder you want to star.

If you want to star multiple files or folders in the same folder, remember you can do that by selecting them, either holding down Ctrl or Shift, selecting them.

Then press "s". A little star will appear next to your file or folder.

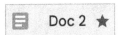

Go to the menu on the left-hand side of the screen and click "Starred".

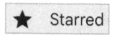

Here, you'll find your starred files and folders for quick access.

If you want to remove them from this filter. Just click on the file or folder and click "s". You will see the star icon disappear.

Home page suggestions

Another way to access your files quickly is to use the suggestions on the Home page. These are files and folders Drive's AI believes you will need.

By default, it will show you files it believes you need and the reason for suggesting them.

Similar to My Drive, you can filter this list, change the view, look at the activity or details of files and folders. You can also take actions on the files and folders, such as share them, download them from here.

Changing the colour of folders

By default, all your folders are a lovely shade of grey.

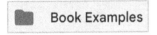

Not the most exciting colour, but that can easily be changed and is useful for quickly identifying the folder you want.

Right click on the folder you want to change. This brings up the menu. Click on "Organize".

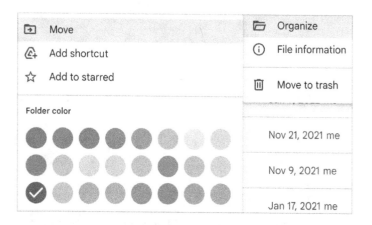

This opens the palette of 24 colours. Just click on the colour you want and it changes the colour of the folder.

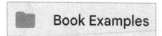

Note: if this is a shared folder, this doesn't change the colour for those who also have access to it. The colours are only seen in your account.

Tip: Colour folders in the same category the same colour. This visually shows they are linked. If you select multiple folders, it will colour all of them at the same time.

Note, if you have a Workspace account, it's not currently possible to colour folders in Shared drives but you can select a theme image.

Shortcuts

Another way to access your files or folders quickly is to create a shortcut to them.

Navigate to the file or folder, then right-click on it to open the menu. Then click "Organize" > "Add shortcut".

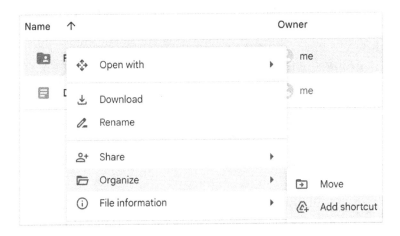

This will then ask you where you want to put the shortcut. This is similar to the Move dialogue box we saw previously. I want to add the shortcut to "My Drive" and Drive has suggested that, so I just click "Add".

In My Drive I can see the shortcut (denoted by a folder with an arrow) has been added.

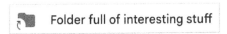

11: Uploading files and folders

Google Drive is not just a place to store your Google Docs, Sheets, Slides, etc but you can use it to store pretty much whatever file you want.

Uploading files

Click on the 'New' button on the left-hand side of the screen, then click on "File upload".

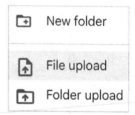

This opens your file directory on your computer. Find your file, and double-click on it.

You can upload multiple files at the same time. Just select the ones you want then click "Open". A little uploading status pop-up window will appear.

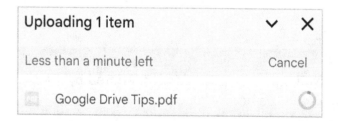

Drive will tell you when the upload has completed. Just click the "X" on the right-hand side to close the status window.

You will see your file in the folder you were in when you added the file(s).

You can upload files to different folders at the same time, although I wouldn't do too many at the same time, as sometimes errors happen. You can locate the files in the folder by clicking on the green circle, which will change to a folder icon and state "Show file location".

You can also drag a file from your file directory directly into Google Drive. Just drag the file across onto your Drive and drop it. The upload status window will then appear as above.

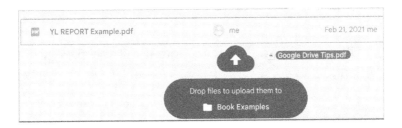

If you've already uploaded a file with the same name, Drive will ask you if you want to replace the original one or keep both files.

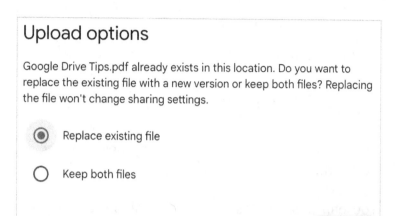

If you keep both, it will add a suffix to the file name.

Uploading a folder of files

You can also upload a complete folder. Click on the New button and choose Folder upload.

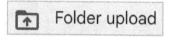

It will check if you want to upload all the files. Click Upload.

Upload 158 files to this site?

This will upload all files from 'Drive-Rev13-Screenshots'. Only do this if you trust the site.

Cancel   Upload

It will tell you the progress of uploading the file, X out of the total number of files.

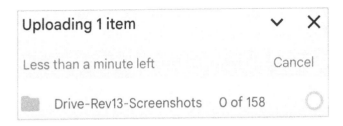

Uploading 1 item   ∨ ✕

Less than a minute left   Cancel

Drive-Rev13-Screenshots   0 of 158   ◯

You can cancel an upload by clicking on the progress circle and clicking the cross.

30 of 158   ✖

To resume an upload that's been cancelled, click on the curved arrow.

12: Downloading your files and folders

Sometimes you need a copy of your files in a place other than your Drive and to do so, you will need to download them.

Downloading non-Google files

e.g. Word docs, PDFs, mp3s, images

Click on the file you want. Then click the "download" icon on the right.

This will download a copy of the file to your computer.

Note - The download icon can also be found in the menu at the top of the files and folders area.

Downloading Google files

i.e. Google Docs, Google Sheets, Google Slides

The process for downloading these is the same, except for **one key difference**. Google files don't really exist as normal 'physical' files like a PowerPoint document. They live in the cloud on your Google Drive. So, to get them back down to Earth, as it were, Google converts them into a Microsoft-friendly file.

Google Docs become Word documents; Google Sheets become Excel files; and Google Slides become PowerPoint slides

So, to download one, as before, click on the file you want, then click on the "download" icon.

This will download a Microsoft-friendly version of the file to your computer.

Downloading a whole folder

If you've got a lot of files to download, one of the quickest ways is to download a whole folder. This downloads the folder as a .zip file, i.e. all your files are put together in one convenient file. Any Google files are automatically converted to Microsoft-friendly ones.

Click on the folder you want and click the "download" icon.

A pop-up window will appear showing you the zipping status. For a few files this takes seconds.

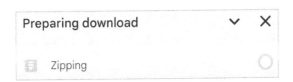

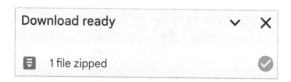

The .zip file is then downloaded to your computer. Drive also adds the date it was downloaded to the filename.

Book Examples-20240104T183636Z-001.zip

On your computer, double click the file to open the contents of the folder.

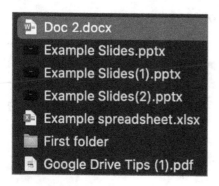

For example, Drive has converted my Google documents to MS ones. It has also downloaded the sub-folder ("First folder") and its contents, which was in the folder I downloaded.

Downloading from within the file - More format options!

When downloading as detailed above, Google Apps are converted into Microsoft files, but with a file open, you also have the option to download the file as other formats. Below are the options you can download your Google Apps as:

Google Slides > PowerPoint (.pptx), .pdf, Image files: .svg, .png, .jpg, or a text file .txt

Google Docs > Word (.docx), OpenDocument .odt, Rich Text Format.rtf, .pdf, .txt, .html zipped, EPUB publication (.epub)

Google Sheets > Excel (.xlsx), OpenDocument .ods, .pdf, .csv, .tsv, .zip

To do this click on "File" then on "Download". You will then see the various formats you can download as. Just click on the one you want.

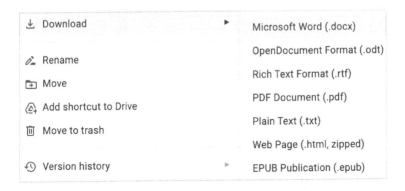

Bear in mind that downloading a document will download that version of the document at that particular time, so any further changes to the original on your Google Drive won't be reflected in the downloaded version.

13: Finding your files

Once you've been using Google Drive for a while, I bet everyone's had that moment where you ask yourself, **"Now, where did I save that file??"**

Or if you're organised like me, you end up with folders within folders within folders, so your files end up nicely hidden away in a folder structure that makes sense, but then ends up taking you ages to get to them.

Well, there's a better way to find them. It's the bar sitting at the top of the screen, with the words "Search in Drive" in it. Just type in the words you can remember and it should find it.

As soon as you click in the empty box, Drive offers you options to filter your search. For example, you may already know it's a PDF you're looking for, so click on "PDFs" so that all the results Drive finds will be PDFs.

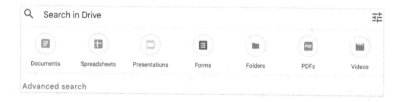

If you click on the filter icon to the side of the box (or Advanced Search), you will open further options to filter your results.

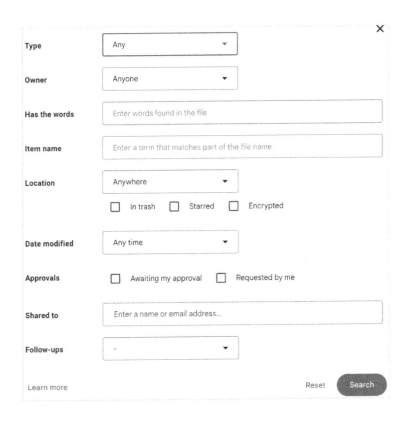

Type: Shows the file type options to filter your search by.

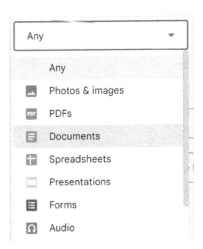

Owner: This gives you options of filtering by the owner of the files.

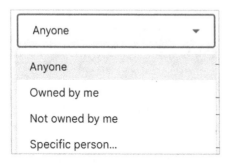

Has the words and **Item name:** Here you can look for files that contain specific words or part of a file name.

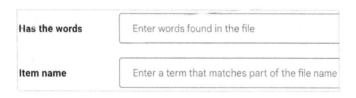

Location: You can state where you want to look in.

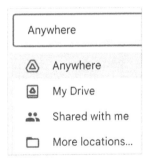

Date modified: This will open up various time options and the option to enter a specific time period yourself (in "Custom...").

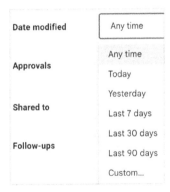

Approvals: You can filter by document approval status.

Shared to: Filter by a user the file or folder was shared with.

Shared to	Enter a name or email address...

Follow-ups: Filter by documents that contain suggestions or actions in the comments.

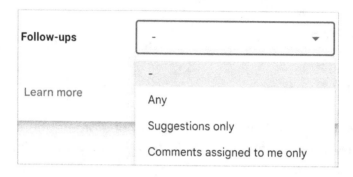

All in all, you should be able to find that file you're looking for!

Within the search box you can also use the same search tricks that you can use in Google's main search engine.

Searches	What it does	Example
Quotes ""	Documents that contain an exact phrase.	"match this phrase exactly"
OR	Documents with at least one of the words.	tacos OR nachos
Minus sign -	Documents that exclude a word. So if you want "salsa," but not "dancing," use...	salsa -dancing

Search within a folder

If the file or folder you're looking for is in a particular folder, you can search just within that folder.

Right-click on the folder and select "File information" > "Search within + the name of the folder".

Under the search bar at the top of the screen you will see the name of the folder. Then type in the file name you're looking for.

14: Working with Microsoft docs

It's possible to upload Microsoft Office (MSO) documents to your Google Drive, they do take up precious space on your Drive and PowerPoint files in particular, can be quite large files.

There are two ways to work with them:

1) Edit them as Microsoft Office documents within the Google interface

2) Convert them to their Google file equivalents (e.g. Word files to Google Docs)

Uploading them to Drive means you can edit and view on any computer and don't need programs like Word installed.

Editing Microsoft Office documents

Double-click on the MSO file you want to edit. In this example, I've got a PowerPoint file on my Drive.

 Example Slides.pptx

This will open the PowerPoint in Slides. Note, that this is still a PowerPoint file and we can see that it has the .PPTX extension next to the filename showing us it's an MSO file.

We can then edit it as an MSO file. The limitation is that we have the options in Google Slides, not the ones in PowerPoint.

Converting Microsoft Office docs to Google ones

To convert it to a Google Slides file, we need to save it as one. Open it as above then click on File and Save as Google Slides.

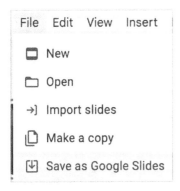

A new tab will open and a copy of the presentation will open, this time as a Google Slides file.

Opening the newly-created Google Slides file, we will see that next to the filename we don't have the .PPTX extension label, showing us that this is a Google Slides file.

93

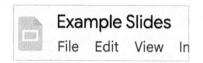

Example Slides

File   Edit   View   In

Back in your folder, you will see two files. The new Google document (here a Google Slides file) and the original MSO document.

Example Slides	me	11:38 AM me		7 KB
Example Slides.pptx	me	Feb 21, 2021 me		435 KB

Note: on the right of the screen, you can see the file sizes. The PowerPoint one was 435Kb and the Google Slides one was just 7kb.

Tip: Generally, the conversions are good, but if your original files had a lot of formatting, animations, etc, it's a good idea to check the new document, to make sure it looks fine, as sometimes, things can go awry.

If you're happy with the conversion, then you may want to delete the original file to save space. Right click on the original file, and from the menu, click "Move to trash".

15: Previewing your files

If you have PDFs, pictures, or other files which aren't Google ones, Google Drive allows you to preview your file right within Drive. This is useful if you want to view those documents without having to exit Google Drive and to open them in an external app.

To open the preview of the file, just double-click on it. Below is an example of a PDF I've opened.

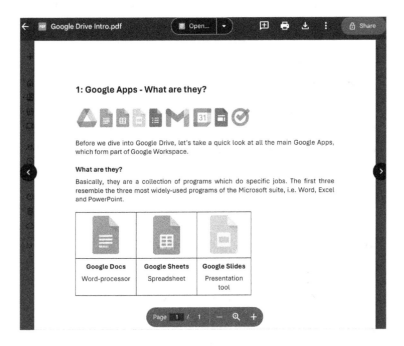

At the top, in the middle, we have the "Open with..." menu, which allows you to open the file in a Google App (e.g. Google Docs) or a Google Add-on.

In the top-right-hand corner, we have some options. Going from left to right:

Add comments: To add comments to the file.

Printer: To open the print dialogue box.

Download: To download the file to your computer.

Three dots: Extra options

Adding comments

To add comments to the document, select the text you want to refer to and then click on the comments icon (either at the top of the screen or to the right of the page).

Enter your comment and click "Comment".

This will then add the comment to the right of the page, with who left the comment and the date and time. Clicking on the tick icon will resolve the comment and hide it.

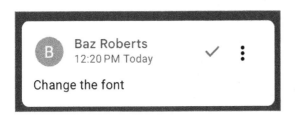

Clicking on the 3-dot menu gives you the option to edit or delete the comment, and also to get a link to the comment, so if someone clicks on the link it takes them straight to it.

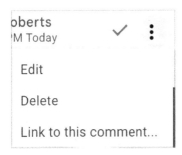

Other options

The printer and download icons I think are self-explanatory.

Clicking on the three dots, gives you the option to move the file, star it for quick access, rename it, search for a specific text, and give you some details about the file.

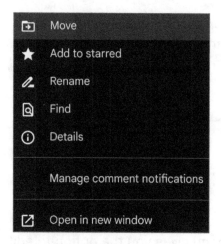

Managing comments

You can manage the comments from here.

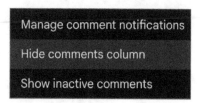

Manage comment notifications – Here you can control whether you receive notifications of all the comments added on this file, comments that have included you (using for example, @ + email address or name), and to turn them off.

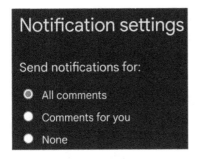

Hide/Show comments column – Hides or shows the comments on the side of the page.

Show/Hide inactive comments – This shows or hides comments that have been resolved. It's good for seeing the history of the comments or if you want to reopen one of them.

To reopen one, show the inactive comments and then click on the blue arrow icon.

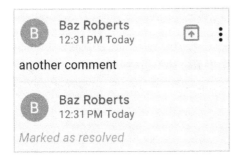

Finally, you can open the file in a new window, which is useful, especially if you want to continue working in your Drive. As it's on its own page, it also displays the file's URL, which can be useful to copy and paste elsewhere.

Note, the URL when the file is initially previewed is this one, which if you look closely, refers to the folder it's in, not the file itself.

`drive.google.com/drive/folders/1teT4sK6FMjrAp0bKhIQRnqVXTqsWd6Jk`

When we open it in its own window, we see it's a file URL, and if we share this, the user will be able to preview the document in its own window.

`drive.google.com/file/d/1FhkvohWI2ZJfHTBuOQTiweQJ0MOns-5w/view`

At the bottom, you have the page number (useful if it's a multiple page document), and the zoom function. Clicking on the magnifying glass automatically zooms the file to the width of the page.

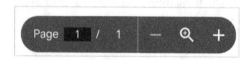

On the side of each preview, you will see arrows, so you can flick through files that are in that particular folder.

16: Settings

In this final chapter, let's take a look at what's in Settings and the overall configurations we can set up.

To access the Settings menu, click on the cog icon in the top-right of the screen and select "Settings".

Here, we have three options.

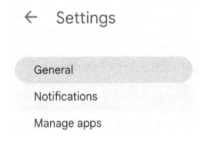

General
Under "General" we can see how much storage we're using, the files that are taking up that space, and the option to buy more storage.

We can also change the default start page from the Home page to your My Drive.

We can also change how much information we see on the screen, by changing the Density option.

Storage

3 KB of 15 GB used

(Buy storage)   (View items taking up storage)

Start page

◉ Home

○ My Drive

Density

○ Comfortable

◉ Cozy

○ Compact

Next, we can choose to automatically convert uploaded MS files to Google documents.

We also have the option to be able to work offline when there is no internet. The changes to the files are then synced once connected again. This can be useful when using a laptop on the move.

We can change the language of our Google Account.

Finally, we can manage our Workspace search history.

Uploads

☐ Convert uploads to Google Docs editor format

Offline

☐ Create, open and edit your recent Google Docs, Sheets, and Slides files on this device while offline

Not recommended on public or shared computers. Learn more

Language

(Change language settings)

Privacy

Manage search history

Search history includes things you searched for in Google Workspace. The searches stored by Google Workspace are used to give you more personalized experiences, including faster searches and more helpful content recommendations

Notifications

Here, you can choose to receive notifications in your browser or email about Google Drive items.

Browser

☐ Get updates about Google Drive items in your browser

Email

☑ Get all updates about Google Drive items via email

You'll still receive messages related to your Google account

Manage apps

This lists the apps that are connected to your Google Drive.

103

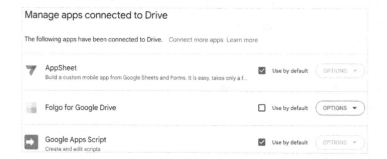

You can control whether you want to use the apps by default or not.

The end or just the beginning?

I hope you've found this book useful and it's given you a good head start into using Google Drive.

FEEDBACK
I would love to hear your thoughts on this book! It would be great, if you could spare a minute to fill in this short feedback form:
bit.ly/BazsBooks

Thank you!
Barrie "Baz" Roberts
Rev15

Some of the other books and ebooks available by this author on Amazon:

Beginner's Guide to Google Sheets	Beginner's Guide to Google Docs	Step-by-step guide to Google Forms

Step-by-step guide to Google Sites	Step-by-step guide to Google Slides	Google Sheet Functions – A step-by-step guide
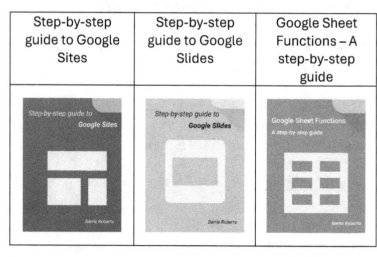		
Google Sheets Functions 2	Step-by-step guide to Google Meet	Beginner's Guide to Google Apps Script 1 - Sheets
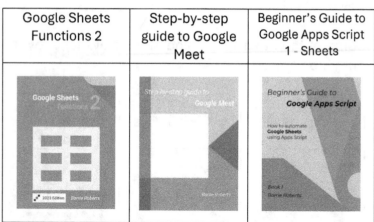		

I also share blog posts and information related to Google Workspace and Google Apps Script on my website www.bazroberts.com, on Medium: **@bazroberts**, on X: **@barrielroberts**, and videos on YouTube: **@bazroberts**